BY **JOSEPH BRUCHAC** · ILLUSTRATED BY **S.D. NELSON**

LEE & LOW BOOKS INC. · NEW YORK

Crazy Horse's
VISION

CRAZY HORSE, they say, was always different. Many children cry when they are born, but not Crazy Horse. He studied the world with serious eyes.

"Look at our son," his mother said. "How brave he is!"

"See how curly his hair is," said his father, Tashunka Witco.

"We will call him Curly," said his mother.

Seasons passed. The boy named Curly grew strong and wiry, but would never be tall. Though small, Curly was a leader. When others spoke, he was quiet. When others hesitated, he acted.

"Follow me," he would say, and the other boys would follow. A Lakota boy could go wherever he wanted and Curly wanted to go everywhere. He led his friends to swim in the river and ride far over the plains. They followed him up the highest cliffs where eagles nested.

"Be brave," he told them. "If we're brave, we can help our people."

When Curly was eleven winters old, his father brought a wild
horse into the camp.

"Whoever is first to ride this horse can have it," announced Tashunka
Witco. Then he and his best friend, High Backbone, went into the tipi to eat.
When they heard shouts they rushed outside to look. Curly was on the back of
the wild horse. It could not throw him. When it finally stood still, Curly slid off,
his arms around its neck.

"Your son has a new horse," said High Backbone.

"So it seems," said Tashunka Witco.

Two summers later, Curly joined the men on a buffalo hunt for the first time. Hunting buffalo was dangerous. If your horse stumbled and you fell, you could get trampled to death. To strike a running buffalo with an arrow was difficult. Even the best hunters often had to shoot several arrows to bring down a buffalo.

As the hunters rode down the hill, the buffalo began to run. Their hooves sounded like thunder. Curly's swift horse carried him ahead of the others. Soon he was in the midst of the herd, next to a huge buffalo. Guiding his horse with his knees, Curly drew back the arrow and let it loose. It went straight and the buffalo fell. When the others caught up to him, Curly was standing by his first buffalo.

"I give this buffalo to all those in our camp who have no one to hunt for them," he said.

Although Curly's life as a boy was good, things were about to change.
Wasichu settlers began to pass through Lakota land. The Army built a fort.
They said it would keep peace between the Lakotas and the whites.

One day a white man's cow strayed into the Lakota camp. It trampled through a tipi and knocked over cooking pots. A warrior stepped forward and killed the cow with an arrow. The settler who owned the cow demanded that the Army punish the Lakota. Chief Conquering Bear tried to avoid trouble. He offered a mule and five horses for the cow.

The white soldiers ignored the offer and fired their rifles and wagon guns at the Lakotas. Conquering Bear was mortally wounded.

Curly was there and witnessed the terrible thing that happened. He was deeply troubled. As he stood by the burial scaffolds, many thoughts went through his mind. What would happen now to his people? Who would defend them? Curly decided he needed a vision to guide him.

Normally a boy would need a holy man to prepare him for
a vision quest. He would fast and purify himself in a sweat lodge
before setting out. But Curly felt he had no time.

Curly rode away from the camp. He went along the bluffs above
the river and came to an eagle-catching pit dug into the soft earth.

Curly tied his rope between the legs of his pinto horse so it
would not wander away. He climbed the hill, stripped off his clothes,
and stepped down into the pit. He sat and prayed for a vision.

The day passed and night came. Curly did not leave the pit. He prayed for strength to help his people. A second day and night passed. Without food or water, Curly continued to pray.

"Wakan Tanka," he cried. "Great Mystery, even though I am small and pitiful, I want to help my people."

Dawn of the third day brought nothing to his eyes or ears. No spirit, no bird, no animal, not even an insect, came to him. All he saw was the sky above and the earth of the pit.

At last, late on the third day, Curly climbed out of the pit. He was barely able to stand. Would a vision ever come to him? Was he unworthy? He staggered downhill to where his pinto grazed near a cottonwood. Reaching the tree, he could stand no longer.

Then the vision came. It was a rider on the back of Curly's
own pony, yet horse and man floated in the air. As the
man rode closer, Curly saw that he wore blue leggings
and his face was not painted. A single feather
hung from his long brown hair. Behind one ear
a round stone was tied. A red-backed
hawk flew above the man's head.
Curly heard these words which
were not spoken.

Keep nothing for yourself.

While the air filled with streaking hail and bullets, nothing touched the rider. Storm clouds rolled above. The thunder sounded, but the man rode on. On the man's cheek was a lightning bolt. Spots like hail were marked onto his chest.

Suddenly many Lakotas were all around the rider. Some seemed to be holding him up while others seemed to be pulling him from his horse.

Curly felt hands on his shoulders, shaking him. He opened his eyes. His father and High Backbone were bent over him, concern in their faces. Curly looked past them. His pony grazed peacefully, hobbled as it had been before his vision began. No rider was on its back. But a red-backed hawk was perched in the top of the bush near his horse.

"Why are you here?" his father demanded.

"I came to seek a vision," Curly said.

Curly wanted to tell them what he had seen, so they could help him understand it. But his father's face was filled with anger.

"You were not prepared," his father said. "How could you do this without going into the sweat lodge? How can you expect a true vision without being guided by your elders?"

Curly looked over at High Backbone. He, too, was angry. They would not listen to him. So he said nothing. He let them carry him back to the camp. He kept his vision in his heart and shared it with no one.

Three winters passed. Curly had become not a different person, but a better one. No young man was more generous or serious. He spoke even less than before, but when he did speak his words were always wise and clear.

Finally, Tashunka Witco saw the time had come to speak with his son about his vision quest. Tashunka Witco sat with Curly in the sweat lodge and listened quietly as Curly described the powerful vision given to him.

"The man on that horse," Curly's father said, "is the one you will become. You will be first to defend your people, though some will try to hold you back. As long as you keep nothing for yourself, no arrow or bullet can hurt you. Because of that vision you must have a new name, so I give you my own. From now on, you will be Tashunka Witco."

The young man, whose name had been Curly, listened to his father's words. His new name fit that vision of a horse dancing through a storm. From that day on he would be known by that name. His name would stand for the bravest of all the Lakotas, one who always defended his people. In the days to come, all the world would know that name as it was said in English. They would know Crazy Horse.

AUTHOR'S NOTE

Some of the most widely known Native peoples of North America are those who call themselves Lakota, but who are also sometimes called Sioux. Seven different nations, or "camp circles," make up the Lakota peoples: the Oglala, Brule, Minniconju, Sans Arc, Blackfoot Lakota, Two Kettles, and Hunkpapa. As the Lakotas fought to defend their lands and families during the 19th century, Crazy Horse stood out as one of their courageous leaders.

Crazy Horse was a quiet man. He said little during his lifetime and died young, but many described him as a military genius, the bravest man in a nation of incredibly brave people. It is said that in keeping with his vision, Crazy Horse owned nothing. Though fierce in war, he was a man of great kindness and always showed compassion for his people. He never wore an eagle feather headdress or elevated himself above others, yet everyone who met him remembered him.

Crazy Horse never told his own story. The best-known book about him, *Crazy Horse, The Strange Man of the Oglala,* by Mari Sandoz, was based largely on the memories of his friend He-Dog, who was very old when Sandoz interviewed him, having outlived Crazy Horse by over 50 years.

Crazy Horse was born in the Black Hills in the Great Plains, in the area close to the border that divides Wyoming and South Dakota, on an autumn day in 1841 or 1842. He was light-skinned and his hair was curly. His parents were Lakota, his father a "holy man," whose name, Tashunka Witco, meant "crazy horse."

When a Lakota boy is born, he is given a name, but that is not the child's name forever. Later on, if the boy performs a brave or important deed, he earns an adult name. Sometimes, as was the case with Crazy Horse, the boy's own father gives up his name to his son. After giving his name to his son, Crazy Horse's father became known as Worm.

At the time Crazy Horse lived, the Lakotas and other Native peoples of the plains were being forced to give up their old ways by the United States. Every treaty they made with the United States government was broken. Again and again, the Indians found themselves cheated and betrayed. Villages that had declared peace were attacked without warning by soldiers such as General George Custer. The irony of Custer's final defeat by Crazy Horse and Sitting Bull at Little Bighorn in June, 1876, was that the battle began when Custer made a surprise attack on yet another village that wanted to be left alone.

How did Crazy Horse die? No gun or arrow struck him down in battle. In September, 1877, Crazy Horse rode into Fort Robinson to talk of peace. Instead, the soldiers tried to throw him into the guard house. Crazy Horse resisted, and two Lakota men, who were now Indian policemen, grabbed his arms to hold him. As Crazy Horse resisted, a white soldier named William Gentiles ran forward and stabbed him with a bayonet.

Some say Crazy Horse made a long speech as he lay mortally wounded, forgiving the Indian agent who had led him into the fort under a flag of truce. This seems unlikely since Crazy Horse was a quiet man. Others say Crazy Horse spoke only three words after he was stabbed: "Hey, hey, hey!" Still others say Crazy Horse spoke to his father, Worm, who was there with him. "Father, I am hurt bad. It is no good for the people to depend on me any longer."

The Indian resistance against overwhelming odds is the stuff of legends. Today, more than a century later, contemporary Native peoples are still inspired by the honor and courage, the generosity and strength, of the men and women of those times. No person is more inspiring than the boy who sought a vision to help his people and became the greatest warrior of all. Though he is dead, his spirit lives on. The people still depend on Crazy Horse.

ILLUSTRATOR'S NOTE

As a member of the Standing Rock Sioux tribe in the Dakotas, my painting has been influenced by the traditional ledger book style of my ancestors. The picture on the endpapers of this book was painted in the traditional ledger book style of the Plains Indians, which include the Lakota people. It shows the Battle of the Little Bighorn, the crowning achievement of the Lakota chief, Crazy Horse.

What is the ledger book style and where did it come from? During the last part of the 19th century, Native peoples were forced onto reservations by the United States government. Some of the strongest resistance to this was among the Plains Indians. As a result, many of their leaders were put in prison, and hundreds of children were sent east to boarding schools to be "civilized." During this time, some Indians were given ledger books in which to draw. These books had lined pages and were intended for bookkeeping. Artists used pencils, pens, and watercolors on the ledger book pages to create bold images of their vanishing culture. Their work was distinguished by outlined two dimensional figures and indistinct facial expressions.

For the Lakota people, colors have special meanings. For example, red represents the east where each day begins with the rising of the sun. Yellow represents the south, summer, and where things grow. I painted Crazy Horse blue because blue represents the sky and a connection with the spirit world.

I included other traditional symbols in my art for this book. Plains Indians often painted themselves, their horses, and their tipis. They believed that doing so gave them special spiritual powers. Warriors used images of lightning bolts and hail spots to represent the awesome power of a thunderstorm. Images of lizards and dragonflies represented speed and elusiveness. Lakota women preferred geometric designs to decorate clothing, robes, tipis, and cradleboards. They used paints, dyed porcupine quills, and their favorite ornament—brightly colored glass trade beads.

In this book, I have not restricted myself to painting in the traditional manner. In some illustrations, I used perspective, color, and texture in more contemporary ways. My intention was to draw young readers into the story. I hope that through my pictures, readers will not only gain a better understanding of Crazy Horse, but an insight into the art of the Plains Indians. All my pictures were painted with acrylics on wooden panels.

Text copyright © 2000 by Joseph Bruchac
Illustrations copyright © 2000 by S.D. Nelson
LEE & LOW BOOKS Inc., 95 Madison Avenue, New York, NY 10016

Printed in Hong Kong by South China Printing Co. (1988) Ltd.

Book design by Christy Hale
Book production by The Kids at Our House

The text is set in Amerigo.
The illustrations are rendered in acrylics on wooden panels.

10 9 8 7 6 5 4 3 2 1
First Edition

Library of Congress Cataloging-in-Publication Data
Bruchac, Joseph.
Crazy horse's vision / by Joseph Bruchac ; illustrated by S.D. Nelson.—1st ed.
    p. cm.
Summary: A story based on the life of the dedicated young Lakota boy who grew up to be one of the bravest defenders of his people.
ISBN 1-880000-94-6
1. Crazy Horse, ca. 1842-1877—Fiction. [1. Crazy Horse, ca. 1842-1877—Fiction.
2. Oglala Indians—Fiction. 3. Indians of North America—Great Plains—Fiction.]
I. Nelson, S.D., ill. II. Title.
PZ7.B8882816 Cr 2000
[E]—dc21   99-047451

Wli dogo wõngan. For all my relations in our many nations—J.B.

In memory of those star-filled nights when the Northern Lights danced for a little boy above the Dakota prairies—S.D.N.

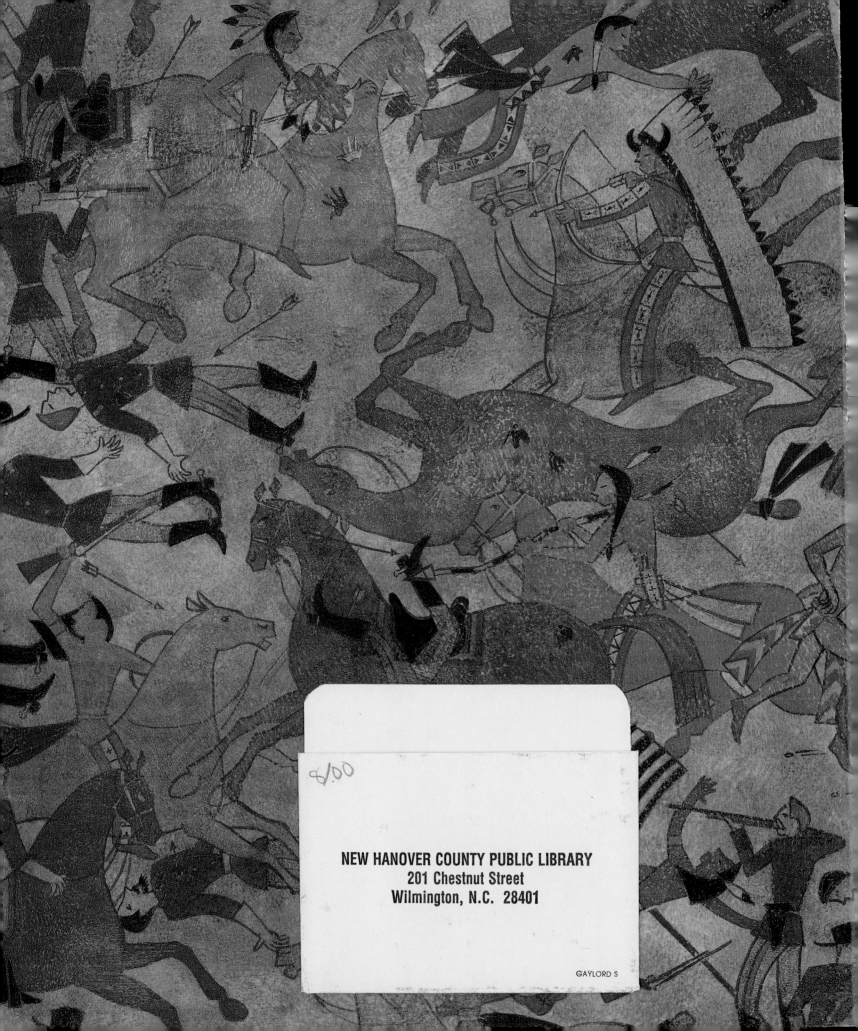